JESUS ROSE FROM THE DEAD:

THE EVIDENCE

JESUS ROSE FROM THE DEAD:
THE EVIDENCE

CATHERINE MACKENZIE

CF4·K

10 9 8 7 6 5 4 3 2
Copyright © 2010 Catherine Mackenzie
ISBN: 978-1-84550-537-0

Published in 2010 and reprinted in 2017
by Christian Focus Publications,
Geanies House, Fearn, Tain,
Ross-shire, IV20 1TW,
Great Britain

Cover design by www.moose77.com
Illustrations by Fred Apps
Printed by Bell & Bain, Glasgow

The author wishes to thank specifically the following people she
has found helpful while writing this book: Lee Strobel (*The Case
for Christ*), R.T. Kendall (*Understanding Theology*), Geisler Brooks
(*When Skeptics Ask*), William Mackenzie (*Resurrection Sermon:
Preached at Kingsview Christian Centre 2009*).

CONTENTS

WHAT IS TRUTH?

'I'm amazing I am! I've just held a lion in one hand while drinking a cup of tea through my nose!'

'That's nothing! I can balance on my little finger and score a basket from 100 metres.'

'Really? I suppose that would be something to shout about if I hadn't managed to climb a skyscraper with my hands tied behind my back, and balancing a bowl of porridge between my knees.'

Do you believe any of these guys? They're all making ridiculous claims so it's pretty easy to see that none of them is telling the truth.

However, what would you say if someone announced on live television, 'I am going to perform the most amazing stunt ever. I will walk across a tightrope hanging above a raging river, and I'll do it blindfolded'? Now that would be amazing! If she was a well-trained acrobat with lots of skill and experience she might be able to do it. But how would you know for sure that she was telling the truth?

People often question things today. Sometimes they are right to have doubts. You shouldn't believe everything you read in the newspapers. Have you noticed how journalists often have to apologise for misquoting someone?

You will smell like a fresh meadow every day...

Sometimes a television programme isn't accurate because it only gives one side of the story. Adverts make ridiculous claims about the products they sell, for example, 'You will smell like a fresh meadow every day when you use Hazy Daisy laundry detergent.'

No wonder people are sceptical about what they read in newspapers and see on television.

If you were to go out into the street with a questionnaire to find out what people thought about truth, you would get a variety of answers. Some people think that the truth doesn't really matter. They think it's alright for one person to believe one

thing and another person to believe something that is opposite to that or contradictory.

But the meaning of the word truth *is* important. Truth is the opposite of lies. Sadly, many people don't believe the truth about Jesus Christ. They believe lies instead. Across the world many people believe in other gods and not the one true God. Have you ever come across this?

Perhaps one morning you go down the stairs for breakfast and you read the front page of your dad's newspaper before he gets to it. There is an article about all the different religions in your country. You read about Hindus who have many different gods and goddesses, you read about Muslims who worship Allah. You see a picture of a Buddhist monk.

Then at lunchtime in the canteen your friend says that there is only one God. He read the following verses at his church.

 BIBLE VERSE Hear, O Israel: The LORD our God, the LORD is one! DEUTERONOMY 6:4

And this is eternal life, that they know you, the only true God, and Jesus Christ whom you have sent. JOHN 17:3

Which one is true? The newspaper or the Bible? Here is your answer – God's Word is the truth! The Bible tells us that Jesus Christ is the Son of God and has been sent by the one true God. God's Word tells us that Jesus rose from the dead. This is the truth and the truth is very important – because if you do not believe the truth then you will believe a lie.

Perhaps you have heard some people say that they don't believe anything. A friend might say, 'I don't follow any religion.' Perhaps they say, 'I don't believe in God, any god at all.' Someone who says they don't believe in anything is mistaken. Human beings always believe in something. It's just that when people turn away from the one true God they worship whatever they think is best – even themselves. Whatever you long for most or give most importance to in your life then that can be described as your god.

Even when we trust in Jesus Christ to save us from our sin we still fall into the trap of putting other things before God. Your whole life needs to be given over to God – not just the leftover bits of your day. So even when you are playing football, spending time with friends, relaxing in front of the T.V., do these things in order to please God and to honour him.

It is a fact that people can make a god out of anything. False gods are called idols in the Bible. False gods have even been made out of wood and metal.

JESUS ROSE FROM THE DEAD

People today make false gods out of intelligence, beauty, money, football teams, singers, film stars. God gives us specific instructions about false gods in the Bible:

BIBLE VERSE

You shall not make for yourself a carved image, or any likeness of anything that is in heaven above, or that is in the earth beneath, or that is in the water under the earth. EXODUS 20:4

In the book of Isaiah, God teaches us how ridiculous it is to worship worthless idols (see Isaiah 44:6-23). A story is told about a craftsman who finds some wood and then chisels some of it while he uses the rest of the wood to make a warm fire. In the flames he bakes some bread and prepares a meal. He warms himself and then turns the rest of the wood into an idol to worship and bow down to.

He looks at the wooden image he has carved and calls out to it, 'Deliver me, for you are my god.' But that bit of carving has no understanding. It can't see or think. The man doesn't stop to consider that this idol he has made is the same thing that he has used to cook his dinner on. The foolish man is worshipping a lie.

The following Bible verses also show how worthless it is to worship anything other than the one true God.

BIBLE VERSE Our God is in the heavens; he does all that he pleases. Their idols are silver and gold, the work of human hands. They have mouths, but do not speak; eyes, but do not see. They have ears, but do not hear; noses, but do not smell. They have hands, but do not feel; feet, but do not walk; and they do not make a sound in their throat. Those who make them become like them; so do all who trust in them. PSALM 115:3-8

It is important to know the truth and worship the one true God. The fact that Jesus came back to life after he died is amazing. When this happened to him it was called the resurrection. It is only someone who has power over life and death that could do that. So it is only God who could have been the power behind the resurrection. Coming back to life after you're dead is a truly amazing event. Jesus Christ did rise from the dead – he came back to life. Being able to raise yourself from the dead is impossible for a normal human being. It is not impossible for God!

You see, Jesus Christ, though he was a human being, was also more than a human being, he was fully human, but without sin and fully God. This was what made Jesus' death on the cross the only effective remedy for sin. It was only the sinless Son of God who could take the punishment for sin. He was raised back to life by the power of God – the only power that can accomplish that amazing miracle.

JESUS ROSE FROM THE DEAD

Now, the only way that you can believe this amazing truth is if God gives you the faith to believe. No number of facts and figures will ever convince you that Jesus is God and that you need your sins forgiven. However, if you are not a believer in Jesus it might be that, when you look at the facts and figures and see how everything ties together, you will realise that the resurrection is not just amazing – it also makes sense! Perhaps God will then open your heart and mind to help you really believe.

If God has already given you a faith to believe in his Son and you have asked God to forgive you for your sins in Jesus' name – then these facts and

figures are going to be useful. This evidence will help you to show others the amazing truth of the resurrection of Jesus Christ.

How much evidence is there to support the resurrection? There is stacks of it. There are eyewitnesses, documents, prophecies and medical evidence, which all support the fact that Jesus died and that he was raised to life again. Different facts from different sources all tie in together to present the truth – the amazing truth – that Jesus rose from the dead.

TURN TO TRUTH TASK ON PAGE 86.

GET ORGANISED

If you don't really know who God is or what happened to his Son Jesus Christ, then you need to read the Bible intro section in this book. It would also help if you read some Bible chapters too. The Bible intro section runs from page 24 to page 36. The Bible chapters that are linked to Jesus' death and resurrection can be found on page 37. The following files on pages 18-23 are short bits of information that you might find useful to know before you start the investigation, but at various points throughout the book you will be prompted to turn back to these pages to look up these files and the Bible intro. If you want to get stuck into the investigation straight away, turn to page 39.

New Word

SCEPTICAL: The word sceptical means to be doubtful about something. For example, if you heard that your brother had cleaned his room you might be sceptical because he'd never done it before. However, if you heard that your mum had promised to make him a chocolate pudding as a reward for cleaning it, then you might change your mind and be convinced.

New Word

PERSPECTIVE: If you have a different perspective, it means you have a different point of view. You see things differently or from a different angle. Two people may describe an incident in different ways because one saw it from the top of the street and the other saw it from an open window. The Gospel writers sometimes differ in what they write simply for that reason.

The Bible

The Bible is unique. It has many writers but one author – God. Every word of it is breathed out by God, or inspired. The different books of the Bible have their own writers – men who took pen to paper or quill to parchment and wrote down the words of God.

Crucifixion

Jesus was put to death by crucifixion – a Roman method of capital punishment where criminals were nailed to a wooden cross. It was a painful way to die. It is from the word crucifixion that we get our word excruciating today. Criminals hung on the cross for as long as it took them to die – this could be hours.

Victim?

Jesus was not a victim. It is wrong to say that if things had turned out differently he would have gone on to live a happy life on earth. God's plan was that Jesus would die for sinners so that sinners could be forgiven and have eternal life. Jesus died willingly on his terms. He *gave up* his spirit.

Is it true?

To tell if something is true or not you need to * Witness it yourself or talk to others who have witnessed it. * Compare their stories to make sure they are consistent. * Research information such as books, internet. * Weigh up the evidence and make a decision.

Forgiveness

God alone forgives sins. He makes a promise to those who trust in Jesus Christ that he will not punish them for their sins. He alone gives eternal life. If we turn away from him when we die we will not have peace. We will face the punishment for our sins. The punishment that we deserve.

God's Son

Jesus is the Son of God. He had a human mother but no human father. Jesus was born because the Holy Spirit came upon Mary and the power of God overshadowed her. God the Son has existed for all eternity. He existed before Mary and became her son in her womb but has always been the Son of God.

Prophecy

In the Old Testament those chosen to bring God's word to the people were called prophets. Their messages often included something that would happen in the future. There are about 60 different prophecies concerning Jesus in the Old Testament. Jesus fulfils them all.

Eyewitness

In a law court, an eyewitness who has seen a robbery is asked what happened. They are questioned about their side of the story. A judge and jury try to decide whether the accused is guilty or innocent. Eyewitness accounts are also important when investigating Jesus' resurrection.

God

There are many religions in the world but only one true God. All other gods are invented by humans to fill their need for something to worship. God shows us what he is like through his Word – the Bible. God is three persons: God the Father, Son and Holy Spirit. One God but three distinct persons.

Sin

Sin is when we do not obey God's commands in thoughts, words or actions. Sin is part of every human from the moment they are conceived. We are so corrupted that that when we are left to your own devices we choose to disobey God rather than to love and obey him.

Consequences

The consequence for unforgiven sin is eternal punishment in hell. Sin has consequences in our day-to-day lives. Sin causes us to hurt others and ourselves. We are in a world that has been corrupted by sin – it is everywhere. TURN TO CONSEQUENCES TASK ON PAGE 88.

God's Actions

God loved the world so much that he sent his son to live a perfect life and take the punishment on himself that sinners deserve. God must punish unforgiven sin. However God can change us so that we love him instead of sin. One day God's people will be changed completely so that they sin no more.

BIBLE INTRO SECTION

BIBLE INTRO: CREATION

In the beginning God created the heavens and the earth. God spoke the world and universe into being. The empty void was filled with a perfect, beautiful creation full of wonderful plants and animals. The first man and woman were created and they were perfect too. There was no sickness, disease, heartache or death. Everything God made was good. (See Genesis 1:10, 12, 18, 21, 25, 31.)

BIBLE INTRO: THE FALL

Adam and Eve lived happily in the garden that God had made for them. They had only one rule to follow – they were not allowed to eat of the tree of the knowledge of good and evil (See Genesis 2:15–17).

The serpent (who was Satan) tricked Eve and she ate from the tree and persuaded Adam to do the same. They both went against God's instructions. Sin came into the world because of Adam's disobedience (See Genesis 3:1-19). This incident is called: The Fall.

BIBLE INTRO: SIN

Adam and Eve faced the consequences of sin: death, disease, spoiled relationships with each other and God. Adam had to work long and hard to grow food. Eve would suffer great pain in childbirth (See Genesis 3:16-19).

However, God promised that a Saviour would come. He would conquer sin and death. The Saviour that was promised is Jesus. Read the next Bible intro to find out more.

BIBLE INTRO: A SAVIOUR WAS PROMISED

There were many years between the first sin and the only Saviour. During that time some people were reminded by God that a Saviour would come. This Saviour would save his people from their sins.

God chose to reveal the truth to the descendents of a man called Abraham. Eventually they came to be known as the Jews. Sometimes they listened to what God told them. Often they didn't. Prophets, priests and kings came and went until eventually a young woman called Mary was visited by an angel. She was told that she was expecting a child. Mary was not married and had never had a relationship with a man, so it was the Holy Spirit that caused her to conceive a baby boy.

Joseph was told to call the child Jesus because that name meant Saviour and he would save his people from their sins (See Luke 1–2).

BIBLE INTRO: JESUS' LIFE

Jesus grew up just like any ordinary little boy did, except for one thing – he never sinned. When he became a man he performed miracles such as healing the sick, giving the blind back their sight, raising people from the dead and many other amazing things.

Check out some of Jesus' miracles in:

Matthew 14: Feeding the 5,000
Jesus walks on water
Mark 10: Bartimaeus receives his sight
Luke 8: Demon-possessed man is healed
A dead girl raised. A sick woman healed.
John 11: Lazarus raised from the dead

BIBLE INTRO: JESUS WAS ARRESTED

The religious leaders didn't believe that Jesus was the Son of God. They criticised him and told lies about him. They even bribed one of Jesus' close companions, Judas Iscariot, to betray him.

With Judas' help Jesus was taken to the religious authorities where he was interrogated, beaten and handed over to the Roman authorities to be crucified. The governor, Pontius Pilate, asked him some questions, but Jesus made very little response, remaining quiet most of the time.

Pilate was the only one with authority in Judea to release prisoners. He tried at first to find some way to let Jesus go free. Because it was a special feast day the people could have their choice of prisoner released. Pilate let them choose between Jesus and a man named Barabbas who was a famous robber. The crowd chose Barabbas. Pilate asked them what he should do with Jesus. The crowd yelled, 'Crucify him.'

BIBLE INTRO:
JESUS WAS NAILED TO
THE CROSS

In order to keep the crowd and the religious leaders on his good side, Pilate agreed to crucify Jesus. He took a bowl of water and washed his hands declaring that he was innocent of Jesus' blood. But a bowl of water wasn't really going to make Pilate innocent of this crime. He had been warned by his wife not to have anything to do with Jesus Christ and the trial, but he paid no attention to her pleas. Barabbas was released and Jesus was led away to be whipped and mocked by the Roman soldiers. After that, Jesus was taken to a place called Golgotha where he was nailed to a cross and left to die.

BIBLE INTRO: JESUS DIED ON THE CROSS

When Jesus was on the cross it was a painful experience, but even then he prayed to his Father God for his enemies (Luke 23:34).

Two thieves were crucified with him. One asked Jesus to remember him when he returned to heaven. Jesus told him that he would be with him in heaven that very day.

On the cross Jesus had to take the sin of his people on himself so that he could die in the place of people who sin against God. This was God's plan. God cannot look on sin and must punish it so he turned away from his one and only Son. Jesus cried out in despair, 'My God, my God, why have you deserted me?' He felt so separated from God that he couldn't even call him Father. Finally he cried out, 'Father, into your hands I commit my spirit.'

Then with a loud cry he called out, 'It is finished!' That was when he gave up his life and died.

BIBLE INTRO: THE BURIAL

The Roman soldiers who were watching the crucifixion did several things. Some laid down bets to see who would get Jesus' clothes. Another heard what Jesus said on the cross and believed that he was the Son of God. Others came to break the legs of the two thieves in order to speed up their deaths. When they looked at Jesus they discovered that Jesus was dead already. Because of that they didn't break Jesus' legs, but they did thrust a spear into his side and out of his body flowed blood and water.

Friends of Jesus later approached Pilate to beg for the body of Jesus. He gave his permission and the body was taken away to be anointed with oils and spices and then wrapped in grave clothes. They took his body to a brand new tomb and laid it there. A stone was rolled across the entrance.

BIBLE INTRO: MARY MAGDALENE

Three days after his death some of the women who were Jesus' followers came to the tomb early in the morning. They discovered that the stone had been rolled away and the tomb was empty. Suddenly two angels appeared and said to them, 'Why do you seek the living among the dead? He is not here, but has risen.'

Mary Magdalene was the first person to actually see the risen Lord Jesus face to face. She was weeping at the time. The angels asked her why she was crying. She replied that Jesus' body had been taken away and she didn't know where it was. Just then she turned round and saw Jesus, but she did not realise who he was. Jesus asked her why she was crying and who she was looking for.

'Sir,' she said, 'if you have carried him away, tell me where you have laid him, and I will take him away.'

Jesus then said, 'Mary' and she knew immediately who he was.

BIBLE INTRO:
THE DISCIPLES

When the disciples heard that Jesus had risen from the dead they didn't believe it. However, Peter and John ran to the tomb to see for themselves. John got there first but didn't go in. As soon as Peter caught up he went inside and saw for himself the strips of linen and the burial cloth. Then John followed. As soon as he saw the empty tomb he believed.

Later, when the disciples were in a locked room, Jesus appeared to them. He showed the disciples his wounds so they would know who he was. One disciple, however, wasn't there. Thomas could not believe that the others had seen Jesus. He insisted that he would only believe if he was able to touch the wounds himself. A week later Jesus appeared to the disciples once again when Thomas was there. As soon as Thomas saw him he believed. He didn't have to touch the wounds of Jesus.

'My Lord and my God!' Thomas exclaimed.

BIBLE INTRO:
ON THE BEACH

On another day Jesus appeared to his disciples while they were fishing by the Sea of Tiberias. They'd been out all night and caught nothing. When they returned to the shore, Jesus called out to them, 'Throw your net on the right side of the boat and you'll get some fish.'

The haul of fish was so heavy they couldn't even pull it onto the boat. John then realised that it was Jesus on the shore. 'It is the Lord!' he declared. As soon as Peter heard him say that he pulled on his coat and jumped into the water. The other disciples followed in the boat. When they arrived, Jesus had some fish cooking for them.

BIBLE INTRO:
JESUS AND THE HOLY SPIRIT

The last time the disciples saw Jesus alive on the earth was when they were on the Mount of Olives. Jesus told them not to leave Jerusalem until they had received the Holy Spirit. After this they would receive power to be witnesses for Jesus throughout Jerusalem and the whole world. Then Jesus was taken up in a cloud to heaven while the disciples watched. Once he was out of their sight the disciples continued to stare upwards. Just then two men dressed in white appeared beside them. They were angels. 'Why are you looking into heaven?' they asked. 'This same Jesus will come back again in the same way that he left.'

So the disciples returned to Jerusalem and waited. Some days later the Holy Spirit came upon them, giving them the power that Jesus had spoken of, and they were able to speak in other languages. They went out into the crowds and began to tell the world about Jesus.

Read This

THE PLOT – Matthew 26:1-5
JUDAS' BETRAYAL – Matthew 26:14-16,
Luke 22:1-6, John 13:18-30
JESUS' ARREST – Matthew 26:47-67,
Matthew 27:11-31; Mark 14:32–15:20,
Luke 22:47–23:25; John 18–19:16
JESUS' DEATH – Matthew 27:45-56,
Mark 15:21-41, Luke 23:26-49,
John 19:17-37
JESUS' BURIAL: Matthew 27:57-66,
Mark 15:42-47, Luke 23:50-56,
John 19:38-42

RESURRECTION: Matthew   28,
Mark 16, Luke 24, John 20 & 21

INVESTIGATE

THE TRUTH

Now it's important to realise that no amount of evidence will ever make an unbeliever into a believer. Seeing the empty tomb did not convince anyone at the time that Jesus was alive. Even those who did see him alive after his death still doubted. It was only God's Holy Spirit who opened up their minds and hearts and made Christ's death and resurrection real to them.

If you present a list of facts about the resurrection this is not going to change someone's heart and make them love God. They're not going to listen to you present the evidence and suddenly say, 'Right, now you've convinced me. I believe it all and I'm going to become a Christian.' It's only the power of

God that can bring about that change in someone's life. But perhaps you're concerned that because you weren't around during New Testament times it's going to be harder for you to believe. That's not true either. Just because you weren't around at the time of the resurrection doesn't mean that you are worse off than the people who saw Jesus for themselves when he rose from the dead.

You can believe in the resurrection too because God's Holy Spirit gives us faith to believe in Jesus. Jesus said that his disciples had seen him and they had believed. But believers in the future who would not see all the wonderful things his disciples had seen would be blessed too (see John 20:29).

To find out about the truth of the resurrection we need to answer the following questions:

1. Did Jesus die?
2. Was Jesus' body stolen?
3. Did people see Jesus after he died?
4. Are there reliable sources?
5. Is Jesus who he claims to be?

So let's look into our first question...

DID JESUS DIE?

Yes. Jesus really did die. He had to die to save his people from their sins. The facts that are available to support Jesus' death are very strong. There are medical facts that clearly prove that Jesus died on the cross – there was no fainting or swooning or faking a death.

Let's imagine that one day you decide to play a trick. Foolishly you pretend to be dead by collapsing on the living room carpet. (Please don't ever do this kind of joke – it's not a good idea!! It's certainly not funny – and someone might not see you lying there and end up stomping on your nose!!!) However, as you lie there between the coffee table and the sofa you hear the doorbell ring. Someone has called a doctor! You're in trouble now! The doctor comes into the living room and starts to give you a check-up. What would he do to determine whether you were alive or dead?

Well, he could check your airway to see if you were breathing. He could also check your pulse to see if your heart was still working. He could look at your eyes or take your temperature. All sorts of things. I suspect it wouldn't take him long before he was suspicious – then he might start poking you – and if you were ticklish then that would be that! Your silly joke would be over and you'd have to cope with a very grumpy doctor.

But say you're not that ticklish – how long do you think you could keep up the act? An hour? Half an hour? Five minutes? I don't think many people could fool a doctor for long. A doctor will definitely know if someone is faking death or not. As you read through the evidence for the resurrection you'll find that even though a modern doctor was not at the crucifixion, there were other professionals there who knew exactly when somebody was dead or not. Who were they? The centurions! There is also plenty of medical evidence in the Bible to prove that Jesus was dead. Even today trained medical professionals recognise the fact that Jesus Christ could not have survived what he went through on the cross.

So the answer to the question 'Did Jesus really die?' is – yes he did. Let's look at the evidence. Jesus was tortured and then crucified. Jesus was whipped by the Roman guards and then he was forced to carry his cross through the streets. Jesus was nailed to the cross and left to die.

So when we look at this list of suffering and torture we can clearly see that even before the crucifixion, Jesus would have been utterly exhausted. Many people would already have died from this treatment before they arrived at the site for their crucifixion. So the very idea that Jesus could survive the cross and torture is highly unlikely.

READ BIBLE INTRO:
JESUS WAS ARRESTED PAGE 29.

Even the night before the crucifixion, Jesus had undergone severe emotional stress which caused him to sweat blood. The whip used by the Roman centurions would have been made of very tough animal sinews and sewn into this would have been pieces of metal and bone. When a whip like that was used on someone's back the skin would be shredded resulting in a huge blood loss.

Then, at a stage when he would have been in great pain and very tired, Jesus had to carry a large wooden cross through the streets. As he did so, he became so exhausted another man was ordered to carry Jesus' cross for him. The exhaustion and physical suffering of Jesus Christ was very real... even before he was nailed to the cross.

READ BIBLE INTRO:
JESUS WAS NAILED TO THE CROSS PAGE 30.

Jesus was not drugged on the cross. He turned down painkillers and he only took a very little wine when offered – not enough to make him pass out.

After this, Jesus, knowing that all was now finished, said to fulfil the Scripture, "I thirst." A jar full of sour wine stood there, so they put a sponge full of the sour wine on a hyssop branch and held it to his mouth. When Jesus had received the sour wine, he said, "It is finished," and he bowed his head and gave up his spirit. JOHN 19:28–30

SEE CRUCIFIXION FACT FILE ON PAGE 18.

When you read Jesus' last words on the cross you realise that these are not the words of someone who has been drugged. It is obvious that he knows what he is saying and what is happening.

Another example of this is when he was able to think about his mother and to see to her care by asking his friend John to look after her.

When Jesus saw his mother and the disciple whom he loved standing nearby, he said to his mother, "Woman, behold, your son!" JOHN 19:26

Jesus' side was pierced with a spear and water and blood gushed out. This is medical evidence that Jesus did in fact die on the cross.

But one of the soldiers pierced his side with a spear, and at once there came out blood and water. JOHN 19:34

JESUS ROSE FROM THE DEAD

The spear pierced his heart which meant that the blood and fluids surrounding the heart were released. This was medical proof that Jesus was dead. But he was dead before that injury took place. How do we know that? Well, the centurions and Roman soldiers are the main witnesses here. It is their testimony that proves Jesus was dead. These men knew how to kill and they knew for sure when someone was dead. So when the Jewish authorities wanted the men to be taken down from the cross the centurions and Roman soldiers made sure that the deaths took place quickly in order that this could happen.

Remember that Jesus was crucified with two criminals. When the centurions and Roman soldiers came up to these two men they were still alive so they broke their legs. This meant that death would be quicker. The men would not be able to raise themselves up on the cross, which they needed to do in order to breathe. So eventually they would die from suffocation. However, when the Roman soldiers came over to look at Jesus they realised that he was already dead so they didn't bother to break his legs.

BIBLE VERSE

So the soldiers came and broke the legs of the first, and of the other who had been crucified with him. But when they came to Jesus and saw that he was already dead, they did not break his legs. JOHN 19:32-33

SEE VICTIM? FACT FILE ON PAGE 19.

The breaking of a criminal's legs was something a Roman soldier always did. It ensured that a criminal died. No soldier would ever risk letting a criminal escape. If that had happened the soldier would have been executed himself. The simple fact that the Roman soldiers did not break Jesus' legs as they usually did is proof that Jesus was already dead.

READ BIBLE INTRO:
JESUS DIED ON THE CROSS PAGE 31.
READ BIBLE INTRO: THE BURIAL PAGE 32.

JESUS ROSE FROM THE DEAD

Jesus' body was then taken down from the cross and embalmed in 100 pounds of spices and bandages. Even if he had woken up in the tomb the weight of the bandages would have made it impossible for him to untie himself. The tomb was also guarded so it was impossible for the disciples or other friends to gain entrance in order to release the body.

BIBLE VERSE After these things Joseph of Arimathea, who was a disciple of Jesus, but secretly for fear of the Jews, asked Pilate that he might take away the body of Jesus, and Pilate gave him permission. So he came and took away his body. Nicodemus also, who earlier had come to Jesus by night, came bringing a mixture of myrrh and aloes, about seventy-five pounds in weight. So they took the body of Jesus and bound it in linen cloths with the spices, as is the burial custom of the Jews. JOHN 19:38-40

So to sum up – Jesus actually died. His dead body really was put into the tomb. That's the truth. Let's go onto the next question.

WAS JESUS' BODY STOLEN?

To investigate this we need to look at the possible culprits. Who might have stolen the body?

THE JEWISH AUTHORITIES
The Jewish authorities would never have stolen the body. Jews did not break the Sabbath day – the special day of rest or holy day. In Matthew chapter 28 we read that the Jewish authorities told the soldiers to accuse the disciples of stealing the body. Why would they have done that if they had the body themselves? If they had indeed stolen it, all they had to do was produce the body in order to prove that Jesus had not risen.

JESUS ROSE FROM THE DEAD

THE DISCIPLES

The biblical account tells us that the guards at the tomb were instructed by the Jewish authorities to say that the disciples had stolen the body while they slept. No self respecting soldier would ever have fallen asleep on duty - it was a death sentence if you were found out. So how come they were able to go around telling that particular story? If it had really happened they would have been executed for it. Did the soldiers see the disciples steal the body? If they did why didn't they stop them? If they didn't see the disciples steal the body then how did they know if that had happened or not? The disciples would not have stolen the body. When you look at these men and what they were like during Jesus' suffering and resurrection, you would notice that they were not brave. All the disciples turned and fled. One even denied that he ever knew him. Few of the disciples were anywhere near Jesus during his crucifixion ordeal. They would not have had the nerve to sneak past the guards and smuggle Christ's body away. They were all in hiding because they were scared of the Jews. Years later these same disciples would be willing to die for the truth of Jesus Christ. It is very unlikely that these men would have been willing to die for something that was a hoax and a lie.

THE POWER OF GOD

The only possible explanation for the empty tomb is the power of God. But how can we present credible evidence for something that happened hundreds of years ago? Relatively easily.

Did you know that when you hold a copy of the New Testament you are holding in your hand one of the most accurate historical documents? It's true. People in universities across the globe recognise that the books of the New Testament are accurate, historical reports.

There is more evidence to support the fact that these events actually took place, than there is for the existence of William Shakespeare and other famous people from history.

To get to the truth we will need to look at eyewitness accounts. So let's investigate the next question: Did people really see Jesus after he died?

SEE EYEWITNESS FACT FILE ON PAGE 21.

DID PEOPLE SEE JESUS AFTER HE DIED?

MARY MAGDALENE AND THE WOMEN
If you were going to accuse the disciples of making up the story of Jesus' resurrection, then the fact that women were the first witnesses to the empty tomb would be a major hurdle to get over. Women were on the lowest rung of the social ladder in New Testament times. A woman wasn't considered to be a very good eyewitness. In a court of law, a woman's testimony simply wasn't accepted.

READ BIBLE INTRO: MARY MAGDALENE PAGE 33.

So if the disciples had made up the story they would not have chosen women as the first witnesses. They'd have picked a man. That would have made the story far more believable to their audience. But in the Gospel accounts we read that it was women who were the first to arrive at the tomb. They were the first to see the empty grave clothes, the first to hear the angels and the first to speak to Jesus himself.

In fact the key testimony is from one woman in particular, Mary Magdalene. Before she became a follower of Jesus she was demon possessed, and it is suggested that she may even have led a very wicked life. If the disciples were going to make up the story of the resurrection they certainly would not have picked a woman who had this sort of reputation.

This is proof that the disciples did not write the story, making it up as they went along. They accurately reported what happened.

SEE IS IT TRUE? FACT FILE ON PAGE 19.

THE DISCIPLES AND OTHERS

When Jesus Christ appeared to the disciples he was able to gain access to their room through locked doors. Walls were no longer an obstacle to him. When he met with the two on the way to Emmaus after breaking bread with them, he simply disappeared.

READ BIBLE INTRO: THE DISCIPLES ON PAGE 34.

However, it is important to note that Jesus wasn't just a spiritual presence. His body was physical. When Jesus met with Mary and then with the disciples they all clung to him in some way. This shows us that Jesus must have had a physical body. Jesus showed Thomas his hands and feet and said, 'a spirit does not have flesh and bones as you see that I have' (Luke 24:39).

TURN TO RESURRECTION TASK ON PAGE 90.

Jesus asked the disciples for some food and on the beach, he ate some fish. This shows that Jesus had a real body.

JESUS ROSE FROM THE DEAD

READ BIBLE INTRO: ON THE BEACH PAGE 35.

The first book of Corinthians, written by the apostle Paul, is where we read that 500 people witnessed Christ's resurrection at the same time. Corinthians is one of the earliest sources. Paul spoke about these 500 people in a way that tells us that he knew many of them. He says that most of the 500 were still living.

Paul mentions these 500 people because he knew that any one of them would willingly answer questions about the resurrection. Paul was certain that these people would back up what he was saying.

 BIBLE VERSE

For I delivered to you as of first importance what I also received: that Christ died for our sins in accordance with the Scriptures, that he was buried, that he was raised on the third day in accordance with the Scriptures, and that he appeared to Cephas, then to the twelve. Then he appeared to more than five hundred brothers at one time, most of whom are still alive, though some have fallen asleep. Then he appeared to James, then to all the apostles. Last of all, as to one untimely born, he appeared also to me. 1 CORINTHIANS 15:3-8

Another proof that Jesus rose from the dead is how this truth changed the lives and the attitudes of the disciples. Look at it this way – after Jesus' death what were the disciples like? They were weak at the knees, scared out of their wits, cowards, and utterly depressed. They were hiding from the Jewish authorities because they were worried that it would be them next.

They'd all had such great hopes for Jesus. They'd hoped that he was going to be the one who would charge in and sort the Romans out – giving Israel back to the Jews. The disciples had hoped that Jesus would sort out all these problems but hadn't understood that the problem Jesus had come to address was their sin and not their Roman enemies. So when Jesus died and all their hopes were squashed, all they could do was run and hide.

But then if you jump a few chapters to the book of Acts you see a change in the disciples. What happened? The disciples became bright and full of hope because the power of the Holy Spirit had come upon them and they had discovered the truth of Christ's resurrection. They had hope – a real, true and eternal hope. They were certain that their sins had been forgiven and that God had given them everlasting life. This certainty gave them the courage to speak out in public about Jesus Christ and what he had done.

READ BIBLE INTRO: JESUS AND THE HOLY SPIRIT. PAGE 36.

Even Peter preached to the crowds. Peter, the man who a few weeks before had denied that he even knew Jesus. What a change! All the disciples were different. Something had happened to them. It was not a hoax of their own making. It was truth.

The disciples had come to realise that Jesus was alive, that he had been raised from the dead by the power of God and that he was the Son of God, the Saviour of the world. They knew that this living Saviour had the power to forgive sins and give eternal life. Sin had been conquered and death was defeated. They had seen the risen Lord Jesus for themselves.

How do we know that that is true? All the evidence we need is their totally changed lives. They were once hopeless cowards – but had been changed to dynamic, courageous witnesses for Jesus. They had faith and it was a faith that they were willing to die for.

SCEPTICS AND FAMILY

Some people think that the New Testament was written by people who had always been friends of Jesus, but this isn't true. Some of the people who wrote books in the New Testament started out as enemies of Jesus. Some took that enmity to the extreme and even tried to kill Christians! What happened to change these people? Something truly amazing – that's what!

SEE NEW WORD: SCEPTICAL FACT FILE ON PAGE 17.

Look at it this way, imagine that you are a professor who believes that the earth is flat. You go around the country giving talks, writing books and arguing with people. You want to persuade others that the earth is flat. Now, would you suddenly change your mind and start saying, for no reason at all, that the earth was round? No, you wouldn't. The only reason you would completely change your mind would be if someone proved to you that you had been wrong.

JESUS ROSE FROM THE DEAD

If someone did prove to you that the earth was round – perhaps by showing you a picture from outer space – then you'd have to change your mind. This change of mind would change your life. You'd probably start writing totally new books about it.

This is just like what happened to some unbelievers in Jesus' time. They started criticising Jesus and fighting against him, only to be convinced they were wrong, very, very wrong. These sceptics or unbelievers were changed. They became convinced of the truth of Jesus Christ.

Let's look at one sceptic named James who was Jesus' brother. In John 7:5 we read that even Jesus' own brothers did not believe in him. But then things changed.

 BIBLE VERSE Then he appeared to James, then to all the apostles. 1 CORINTHIANS 15:7

The risen Jesus appeared to James who later wrote the Epistle of James which is in our Bibles today.

 BIBLE VERSE James, a servant of God and of the Lord Jesus Christ. JAMES 1:1

This verse says that James was a servant of God and of the Lord Jesus Christ. He is definitely no longer an unbeliever!

BIBLE VERSE All these with one accord were devoting themselves to prayer, together with the women and Mary the mother of Jesus, and his brothers.
ACTS 1:14

So Jesus' family testified to the fact that their brother had risen from the dead. Someone had changed them. The brothers who had been against him at the start, believing that he had lost his mind, now knew that he was exactly who he claimed to be. God's Holy Spirit had opened their hearts and minds to the truth.

If Jesus had not risen from the dead then someone like James would never have changed his mind. He would never have come to worship his brother as his Lord and Saviour. Families can often be your best supporters or your worst critics, but this particular critic was changed to a believer and follower of Jesus Christ.

Then of course there was Paul (or when we first meet him – Saul). He became a believer during a very dramatic meeting on the road to Damascus.

Saul had spent a lot of his time searching out Christians to kill and imprison. He was even present at the execution of Stephen. He wasn't throwing the stones, just guarding the coats belonging to the stone-throwers. His presence would have been an encouragement to the men putting Stephen to his death. However, Saul the Christ-hater and Christian-killer was to undergo a complete transformation.

As he set off to Damascus in order to capture more Christians, Jesus appeared to him. A blinding light came from heaven and Saul heard Jesus speak. 'Saul, Saul, why are you persecuting me?' After that, Saul changed, that's the only way you can describe it. It wasn't just his name, it was his whole heart and mind.

A man called Ananias was told by God in a dream to go and speak to him. Ananias was flabbergasted, 'But that's the man who has been causing all that trouble for your people in Jerusalem, Lord!' However, Ananias did as he was told. God had given him very specific instructions – even down to the address that he had to go to.

Eventually, Paul became a great teacher and evangelist. He travelled to many countries to tell people about Jesus Christ. He wrote encouraging letters to the Christians he had once persecuted.

The only reason to explain why a bitter enemy of Christ would change to become one of his greatest supporters is that the resurrection is true and that God is behind it all.

God raised Jesus from the dead. God changed the disciples from cowards into courageous witnesses. God changed the enemies of Christians into those who believed and loved the risen Lord Jesus.

SEE FACT FILES ON GOD, SIN, CONSEQUENCES AND GOD'S ACTIONS ON PAGES 22–23.

ARE THERE RELIABLE SOURCES?

One of the most important sources of information that we have about Jesus and the resurrection is the Bible itself.

The first four books of the New Testament are called Matthew, Mark, Luke and John. These were written by people close to Jesus or close to the eyewitnesses to his life and resurrection. Matthew and John were both disciples. Luke was a close friend of Paul and had access to a lot of the early church believers. Mark was also a follower of Christ and had access to Peter. Each of the Gospels was written within 100 years of the events having taken place. Many people who saw these events at first hand would have been interviewed for their first-hand knowledge.

JESUS ROSE FROM THE DEAD

One clear piece of evidence that we come across in the New Testament is how the church reacted. The new believers were brave and knew what they believed in. Even though they were facing dreadful persecution they showed the world that they believed in the risen Lord Jesus.

The church changed their day of worship, which would have been quite an upheaval for them. Before they became Christians they had always worshipped on the seventh day of the week, or Sabbath day. It was the day that Jews spent in worship of God. However, the Christians knew that the importance of the resurrection day had to be acknowledged. So they changed their day of worship from the seventh day to the first day of the week – the day that Jesus had risen from the dead (Acts 20:7).

Some people, however, have a problem with the New Testament, particularly the Gospels, because there are differences between the accounts of the different writers. Should this really cause you that much trouble? No, not at all. Eyewitnesses often see things differently. This is because they have what is called a different perspective. They see things from a different angle.

SEE NEW WORLD PERSPECTIVE FACT FILE ON PAGE 17.

Look at it this way... several people in your class are asked to write a story about a guy called 'John'.

You write a story about how you walk to school every day with him and that he enjoys football. Now someone else in your class says, 'I cycle to school with John every day and he plays rugby.' Are one or both of these stories wrong because they differ?

Well, a bit of investigation might show that both stories are true. John cycles part of the way to school with this other friend until they get to the bottom of your road. When he arrives, John gets off his bike and pushes it along while he walks beside you into school. He really does enjoy sport but the football team and the rugby team have practice sessions on the same evening. At the beginning of the term, John had to choose which sport to focus on. He enjoys football, but he is better at rugby. So you and the other person in your class could write two different stories about the same person. They only differ because you both have different perspectives.

Now if you were in a court of law and all the witnesses said exactly the same thing, you would think that they were either reading their stories out of a book or they had got together beforehand to compare their stories. That's one of the things that lawyers look out for when they listen to eyewitnesses.

SEE FACT FILE: EYEWITNESS ON PAGE 21.

The slight differences, between the accounts in Matthew, Mark, Luke and John do not mean that these accounts are inaccurate. What matters is that they are all the same in the crucial points. Where it really matters Matthew, Mark, Luke and John are saying the same thing. And the small differences, funnily enough, are a good indication that the Gospel writers did not cook up their stories, but actually told the truth.

Another amazing thing about the Gospels is that, if these accounts were fiction, then the people who wrote them could have written better stories about themselves. If they were going to make up a story about Jesus Christ who rose from the dead they could have at least made it up so that they turned out as the heroes of the story.

If you were going to write a story about yourself that was going to be read in tomorrow's newspaper, you'd be tempted to say all the good things and to brush over the bad things. I'm sure you would.

However, the disciples didn't, because they knew it was important to tell the truth. They had to say it exactly as it happened and as God directed them. So we read about how the disciples were squabbling and cowardly and how they let Jesus down and weren't there for him when he needed them most. The Gospels of Matthew, Mark, Luke and John are rather embarrassing for the disciples. We can be sure then that what we read in these Gospels is a genuine account of what happened. If it was fiction, the disciples would have written a much 'better' story for themselves.

SEE FACT FILE: THE BIBLE ON PAGE 18.

Another explanation for the differences we find between the Gospels is the fact that each different writer has his own style. For example, in an English class if you write a story it will be different to the story written by the person who sits beside you, even if you are writing about the same subject. Perhaps you like to write long, exciting adventure stories but your friend prefers to write brief articles with lots of facts. That means you have different writing styles. Matthew, Mark, Luke and John were the same. In fact every writer in the Bible, from Genesis to Revelation, has his own individual style.

God let that happen. In the Bible, a book written by a gifted poet sounds different to someone who taught the law, or who was a shepherd. However, each writer was given their words by God and it shows. There is a unity to the Bible which could not have been achieved if it had just been written by a collection of different men over hundreds of years.

For example, throughout the Old Testament prophets were given messages from God about things that would happen in the future. Many of these prophecies have come true; many of the prophecies were about Jesus Christ and they came true. Some of these prophecies were specifically about the resurrection of Jesus Christ.

SEE FACT FILE: PROPHECY ON PAGE 21.

However, could Jesus have fixed it so that his life and death met all the predictions made in the Old Testament? The answer is no. Some predictions would have been impossible to arrange. Jesus couldn't have picked where he was born. He couldn't have arranged all the details regarding his death. Was it just a coincidence then that Jesus fulfilled all these prophecies? Could other people have fulfilled them? Well, a brainy mathematician has worked out what the chances are for one person to fulfil just eight of the 60 prophecies that Jesus has fulfilled. The chances that another person could do this would be one in a hundred, million, billion. There's your answer!

Here is one Bible prophecy that refers directly to Christ's resurrection – and it was written many hundreds of years before the birth of Christ.

BIBLE VERSE For you will not abandon my soul to Sheol, or let your holy one see corruption. PSALM 16:10

JESUS ROSE FROM THE DEAD

This refers to the 'holy one' which is Christ and how he would not be left to decay in the grave. His body was transformed and brought back to life. But there is one other chapter in the Bible that is full of amazing prophecy about the Lord Jesus Christ.

In Isaiah chapter 53 you can read several verses that are direct prophecies about Jesus' life, death and resurrection.

BIBLE VERSE

He was despised and rejected by men; a man of sorrows, and acquainted with grief; and as one from whom men hide their faces he was despised, and we esteemed him not. ISAIAH 53:3

This is a description of Jesus Christ. He was despised by his own people. It was the Jewish authorities who sought to have him arrested. When Pilate gave the Jews the opportunity to release Jesus and have a known criminal crucified, the crowd chose the criminal rather than Christ. Pilate asked what he should do with Jesus and the mob yelled back, 'Crucify him.'

READ BIBLE INTRO: JESUS WAS ARRESTED. PAGE 29.

Jesus was even rejected by his closest friend. One man who had been with him as he travelled around the country preaching and performing miracles, betrayed him to the authorities.

Judas Iscariot's name has gone down in history for all the worst reasons. His name reminds people of treachery and deceit. It was Judas who led the soldiers to Jesus. He even showed them who Jesus was by greeting him with a kiss of friendship (See Matthew 26:49). Jesus definitely was a man of sorrows and acquainted with grief.

BIBLE VERSE Surely he has borne our griefs and carried our sorrows; yet we esteemed him stricken, smitten by God, and afflicted. But he was wounded for our transgressions; he was crushed for our iniquities; upon him was the chastisement that brought us peace, and with his stripes we are healed. ISAIAH 53:4-5

This is a prophecy about Christ's saving work on the cross. Although we know that it was Roman nails that pierced Jesus' hands and feet and that it was a Roman cross that he hung on – the final death of Jesus Christ only took place when he agreed to it. He gave himself up to death (See Matthew 27:50; Ephesians 5:2). And he only did this when the full punishment for sin had been laid on him. Who was it that laid this punishment on Jesus? It was God the Father.

Jesus was wounded for our transgressions – our sins. The wounds and bruises he suffered were because of our disobedience to God. He was chastised or punished so that we could have peace with God.

He was whipped and hurt so that we could be healed from sin.

The reason that Jesus died on the cross is so that sinners can come to him, repenting of their sin and trusting in the power of God to save them and give them eternal life. It is only through Christ's sacrifice on the cross that the guilt of sin can be washed away. The power of sin and death were defeated at the cross. Sinners who believe in the Lord Jesus Christ as their Saviour, can look forward in hope to a day when they will be totally free of all sin, every last bit, and they will live in peace with God forever.

BIBLE VERSE All we like sheep have gone astray; we have turned – every one – to his own way; and the LORD has laid on him the iniquity of us all. He was oppressed, and he was afflicted, yet he opened not his mouth; like a lamb that is led to the slaughter, and like a sheep that before its shearers is silent, so he opened not his mouth. ISAIAH 53:6-7

In Bible times most people lived and worked on the land. They knew about sheep and shepherds. The scene described in this verse is of sheep being silent when having their fleeces removed. This would have been a familiar sight to the Jewish people then. They would often have seen lambs being killed. The people at that time would have seen lambs being killed for eating but they would also have taken a lamb to the temple for the annual sacrifice. However, these verses are more than just descriptions of farming practices, they are prophecies that Jesus fulfilled when he suffered at the hands of the Jewish and Roman authorities.

When he stood in front of Pilate he said nothing, even when given the opportunity to free himself from the dreadful death that lay before him. He said nothing because he knew that he had to go through this suffering and death, so that his people could go free.

He knew that he was being punished for the sins of others, so he could not say anything. He could not go free, because then his people would stay in the power of sin and death.

JESUS ROSE FROM THE DEAD

BIBLE VERSE By oppression and judgment he was taken away; and as for his generation, who considered that he was cut off out of the land of the living, stricken for the transgression of my people? And they made his grave with the wicked and with a rich man in his death, although he had done no violence, and there was no deceit in his mouth. ISAIAH 53:8-9

Here we read a direct prophecy of how Jesus was to be buried with the wicked and a rich man. His body would be laid in the tomb, in the same way that a normal sinful human being was buried. But there is a specific mention here made to ' a rich man'. What does that mean?

In the Gospel of Matthew chapter 27 verse 57, we are told that there came 'a rich man from Arimathea', named Joseph, who himself had also become a disciple of Jesus. This man went to Pilate and asked for the body of Jesus. Then Pilate commanded the body to be given to him. Joseph buried Jesus' body in his own tomb – and so another prophecy was fulfilled.

BIBLE VERSE Yet it was the will of the LORD to crush him; he has put him to grief; when his soul makes an offering for guilt, he shall see his offspring; he shall prolong his days; the will of the LORD shall prosper in his hand. Out of the anguish of his soul he shall see and be satisfied; by his knowledge shall the righteous one, my servant, make many to be accounted righteous, and he shall bear their iniquities. Therefore I will divide him a portion with the many, and he shall divide the spoil with the strong, because he poured out his soul to death and was numbered with the transgressors; yet he bore the sin of many, and makes intercession for the transgressors. ISAIAH 53:10-12

This prophecy tells us that it was God the Father who put the punishment for sin on Jesus. Jesus was 'numbered with the transgressors' – he was crucified with two criminals. When he died on the cross he 'bore the sin of many' and stood in the place of sinners – taking their sin and giving them righteousness.

However, these verses also show that his death would not be the end. 'I will divide him a portion with the many,' 'He shall divide the spoil with the strong.' There would be life and glory afterwards. And this is exactly what happened. Jesus Christ rose from the dead and the church of Christ has grown from strength to strength. Nothing has stopped it. One day in the future everyone who has ever existed and who ever will exist shall bow to Jesus Christ. This prophecy has yet to be fulfilled – but it's just a matter of time before all God's prophecies about Christ will take place.

TURN TO PROPHECY TASK ON PAGE 92.

JESUS ROSE FROM THE DEAD

Jesus Christ's Testimony

Within the Bible we also have the testimony of Jesus Christ himself. Throughout his teaching he predicted that he would be raised from the dead. Here are the Bible verses that prove this:

BIBLE VERSE Jesus answered them, "Destroy this temple, and in three days I will raise it up." JOHN 2:19

For just as Jonah was three days and three nights in the belly of the great fish, so will the Son of Man be three days and three nights in the heart of the earth. MATTHEW 12:40

And he began to teach them that the Son of Man must suffer many things and be rejected by the elders and the chief priests and the scribes and be killed, and after three days rise again. MARK 8:31

No one takes it from me, but I lay it down of my own accord. I have authority to lay it down, and I have authority to take it up again. This charge I have received from my Father." JOHN 10:18

Other Sources

Now, the Bible is our most important source of information concerning Jesus Christ and the resurrection, but there are also other sources that we can turn to that in some way back up what we read in the Bible. During New Testament times there were historians who reported on the life and death of Jesus Christ. However, these men were not followers of Jesus – they were what we call secular historians.

The following historians wrote about Jesus Christ and testified to the truth of his life and death: Josephus; Suetonius; and Pliny the Younger. The Jews also wrote about Jesus Christ. So to say that the only source for information about Jesus and the resurrection is the Bible isn't true. The important thing to realise is that although some of these non-Christian historians make reference to the Lord Jesus and his life, death and resurrection, the most important source and the most reliable one is the Bible, the Word of God.

IS JESUS WHO HE CLAIMS TO BE?

Colossians 2:9 explains that Jesus is God and man: 'For in him the whole fullness of deity dwells bodily'. These other verses also say that Jesus is God.

BIBLE VERSE

I am the resurrection and the life. JOHN 11:25
Jesus is God because he has power over life and death.

I am the light of the world. JOHN 8:12
Jesus is God because he gives spiritual light to a sinful world.

I and the Father are one. JOHN 10:30
He is God because God the Father and God the Son and God the Holy Spirit are one God.

JESUS ROSE FROM THE DEAD

I am the way, and the truth, and the life. No one comes to the Father except through me. JOHN 14:6

He is God because he is the only way to God.

Whoever has seen me has seen the Father. JOHN 14:9

Jesus and God the Father are one God, but different persons. When you read about Jesus you are reading about God.

SEE FACT FILE: GOD'S SON ON PAGE 20.

Look at all the things Jesus did in the Bible. We read about his miracles, his power and authority.

READ BIBLE INTRO: JESUS' LIFE ON PAGE 28.

Jesus demonstrated his power in so many ways – over sickness, death, nature. Jesus definitely did these miracles. This is a truth that is backed up by the Bible and by other historical sources. These miracles could only have been done because he had God's power – because he is God.

Jesus also proved that he is God because of how he fulfilled the prophecies of the Old Testament. In the Bible there are prophecies about Jesus' birth, life, death and resurrection. Jesus fulfils them all.

SEE FACT FILE: PROPHECY ON PAGE 21.

WHAT IS IMPORTANT?

The resurrection is vitally important. You can read about the facts and sit back and think about how amazing it is – but do you realise how important it is that Jesus rose from the dead?

1. The fact that Jesus Christ rose from the dead shows that there is someone stronger than death. When someone who trusts in the Lord Jesus Christ is facing death they can say with confidence, 'O death where is your victory? O death where is your sting?' (1 Corinthians 15:55). They can say this because they know that Jesus Christ has conquered death and the grave. This gives them hope for an eternal life after their physical death and freedom from sin and its consequences.

2. Without the truth of the resurrection there would be no reason to believe in Jesus or that he has the power to save us from sin. Look up 1 Corinthians 15:17. If Jesus Christ was not raised from the dead then there is no hope for us to be raised from the dead. Without the resurrection there is no hope for the future.

3. Because Jesus Christ was raised from the dead this means that he is now in heaven interceding for those who trust in him. He is there already speaking to God the Father on their behalf. This means that those who believe in Christ can no longer be condemned. 'If God is for us, who can be against us?' (Romans 8:31).

4. Those who trust in Jesus will one day have transformed resurrection bodies like his, and all because of his resurrection from the dead. Look up these Bible verses: Philippians 3:21; 1 Corinthians 15:49; 1 John 3:2; Isaiah 26:19.

5. Jesus went through so much for sinners. Now he has been glorified in his resurrection from the dead. The Bible tells us that one day 'we will all stand before the judgment seat of God. For it is written: "As I live, says the LORD, every knee shall bow to me, and every tongue shall confess to God"' (Romans 14:10–11).

So from one important thing to another, and this time it is a question that you have to answer. Who do you say that Jesus is? There are only two answers that you can give – you either say, 'He is my Saviour,' or you can say, 'He isn't my Saviour'. You either say, 'I believe in him,' or you say, 'I don't believe in him'.

Those who believe that Jesus is the Saviour of sinners and who trust in him to save them from their sins, will experience a resurrection of their own bodies after their death. On the final Day of Judgment they will be given transformed bodies to live for ever with God. Those who don't believe that Jesus is the Saviour of sinners and turn away from him, will also experience a resurrection – but this will not be a resurrection for eternal life. They will be raised to spend eternity in hell.

SEE FACT FILE: FORGIVENESS ON PAGE 20.
SEE FACT FILE: GOD'S ACTIONS ON PAGE 23.

Your answer to the last question is the most important question of your life. Do I believe in the risen Lord Jesus Christ or not? If you do believe in him and believe that he has risen from the grave, you must take this message to the world, your world. A truth like this can really change things, but first and foremost you must be sure that the truth of Jesus Christ has changed you.

TRUTH TASK

KNOWING WHAT IS TRUE AND WHAT IS NOT IS AN IMPORTANT PART OF LIFE. LOOK AT THE FOLLOWING FACTS – SOME ARE TRUE AND SOME ARE FALSE. CAN YOU WORK THEM OUT? THE ANSWERS ARE ON PAGE 94. SOME OF THESE FACTS ARE IN THE PICTURE – SEE IF YOU CAN FIND THEM.

1. The sun rises in the east.

2. Winter is cooler than summer.

3. If you drop something it falls down.

4. The Arctic is in the south.

5. The sun orbits around the world.

6. Water always boils at 100 degrees centigrade.

7. Jesus Christ died and came back to life.

CONSEQUENCES TASK

WHAT ARE THE CONSEQUENCES TO THESE ACTIONS?
WHAT CONSEQUENCES CAN YOU SPOT IN THE
PICTURE?

1.   Touching a hot pan.

2.   Cutting your finger.

3.   Dropping a ball.

4.   Mixing eggs, flour, sugar and butter.

5.   Putting a pan of water on top of a fire.

6.   Breaking the speed limit.

7.   Letting go of a balloon.

8.   Sin.

The answers are on page 95.

RESURRECTION TASK

TAKE OUT YOUR BIBLES AND COMPLETE THE FOLLOWING TASK. HERE WE HAVE THE TWELVE RESURRECTION APPEARANCES. MATCH THE CHARACTERS TO THE BIBLE REFERENCES ON THE NEXT PAGE.

Mary Magdalene

The other women

Simon Peter

Two disciples

Eleven apostles

Thomas and other apostles

Seven apostles

All the apostles

More than 500 other followers

James

Paul

The Bible references:

Acts 1:4–9

John 20:11

1 Corinthians 15:7

Luke 24:13–32

John 21:1–3

Matthew 28:9–10

Luke 24:34

1 Corinthians 15:8

1 Corinthians 15:6

John 20:26–30

Matthew 28:16–20

PROPHECY TASK

TAKE OUT YOUR BIBLES AND COMPLETE THE FOLLOWING TASK. MATCH THE PROPHECIES ON THIS PAGE WITH THE CORRECT BIBLE VERSE OR VERSES FROM THE NEXT PAGE.

The Messiah would be born of a virgin.

The Messiah would be one of Abraham's descendants.

The Messiah would belong to the tribe of Judah and the House of David.

The Messiah would be born in Bethlehem.

The Messiah would be anointed by the Holy Spirit.

The Messiah would perform miracles.

The Messiah would cleanse the temple.

The Messiah would be rejected by the Jewish people.

At his death the Messiah would be mocked.

At his death the Messiah would be pierced.

At his death people would gamble over his clothes.

The Messiah would rise from the dead.

The Messiah would rise into heaven.

Isaiah 35:5–6; Matthew 9:35

Psalm 22:16; Luke 23:33

Genesis 12:1–3; Genesis 22:18; Matthew 1:1

Psalm 68:18; Acts 1:9

Genesis 49:10; Luke 3:23; Hebrews 7:14

Isaiah 11:2; Matthew 3:16–17

Psalm 16:10; Mark 16:6; Acts 2:31

Malachi 3:1; Matthew 21:12

Psalm 118:22; 1 Peter 2:7

Isaiah 7:14; Matthew 1:21

Psalm 22:7–8

Micah 5:2; Matthew 2:1; Luke 2:4–7

Psalm 22:18; John 19:23–24

TASK ANSWERS

Truth Task Answers:

Well, some of these statements are false. The arctic is in the north; the sun does not orbit round the world – in fact, the world orbits around the sun. Water, funnily enough, does not always boil at 100 degrees centigrade. If you live in a place that is at high altitude, water will boil lower than 100 degrees centigrade.

Some of these statements are true – the sun rises in the east, winter is cooler than summer, if you drop something it will bounce and Jesus Christ really did die and come back to life.

Consequences Task Answers

Here are the consequences to those actions:

You get burnt	You bleed
It bounces	You make a cake
The water boils	The police catch you
It flies away	Death

There are always consequences to actions. If you break the speed limit you can get caught and fined by the police. If you cut your finger it bleeds. Sin has consequences too. The Bible says that 'the wages of sin is death, but that the gift of God is eternal life in Christ Jesus our Lord' (Romans 6:23).

CHRISTIAN FOCUS PUBLICATIONS

Christian Focus | Christian Heritage | CF4K | Mentor

Christian Focus Publications publishes books for adults and children under its four main imprints: Christian Focus, CF4K, Mentor and Christian Heritage. Our books reflect our conviction that God's Word is reliable and Jesus is the way to know him, and live for ever with him.

Our children's publication list includes a Sunday School curriculum that covers pre-school to early teens, and puzzle and activity books. We also publish personal and family devotional titles, biographies and inspirational stories that children will love.

If you are looking for quality Bible teaching for children then we have an excellent range of Bible stories and age-specific theological books.

From pre-school board books to teenage apologetics, we have it covered!

**Find us at our web page:
www.christianfocus.com**

CF4•K
*Because you're never
too young to know Jesus*